BIG ENGLISH STARTER

Linnette Ansel • Lisa Broomhead

Mario Herrera • Christopher Sol Cruz

PUPIL'S BOOK

Contents

Values	Phonics	I can ...
Help your family. I help my (grandma).	**a, e** ant, apple, act elf, egg, elk	... talk about family. ... help my family.
Be polite. Sorry! It's OK. Thank you. You're welcome.	**l, t, i** leaf, look, lake taxi, toy, ten igloo, insect, in	... ask and answer about toys. ... talk about birthday parties and locations around town. ... speak politely.
Mind your manners. Close your mouth. Use a napkin. Say, 'please'.	**n, o, r** nine, nurse, nut on, ox, olive read, rabbit, rug	... talk about foods I like and don't like. ... talk about healthy and unhealthy foods. ... identify good table manners.
Keep clean. Wash your hands. Brush your hair/teeth.	**m, u, k** mouse, map, moon uncle, under, umbrella, king, key, kite	... talk about my body. ... describe how to wash my hands. ... brush my teeth and hair.
Don't throw rubbish. Put rubbish in the bin. Don't throw rubbish. Pick up rubbish.	**y, s, d** yoghurt, yak, yo-yo sock, sofa, seal dad, dish, desk	...ask and answer about actions. ... talk about vehicles and places around town. ... help keep the environment clean.
Follow park rules. Don't pick the flowers. Don't walk on the grass. Don't drop litter Don't feed the birds.	**b, g, z** boy, ball, bed girl, guitar, gate zebra, zoo, zip	... ask and answer about playing at the playground. ... describe a tree in different seasons. ... help keep the park clean.
Recycle clothes. Give away old clothes. Reuse old clothes. Recycle old clothes.	**c, p, h** corn, cat, car park, path, pond hat, horse, head	... ask and answer about clothes. ... describe the weather. ... talk about jobs and uniforms.
Stay safe. It's safe/dangerous.	**v, f, j** van, vase, vest fox, face, fur jar, jam, jump	... talk about different rooms and ask where people are. ... describe the material things are made of. ... stay safe at home.
Respect animals Don't feed the animals. Don't climb the fence. Don't throw rubbish. Don't touch the animals.	**q, w, x** queen, quilt, quick worm, water, wig ox, fix, box	... talk about animals and their abilities. ... say where animals live. ... say zoo rules.

Welcome to class!

 3 Listen and say. Act.

Listen, look and say.   **Listen and chant.**

1	**2**	**3**	**4**	**5**
6	**7**	**8**	**9**	**10**

6 Listen and find. Ask and answer.

1

2

7 **Listen, look and say.**   **8** **Listen and chant.**

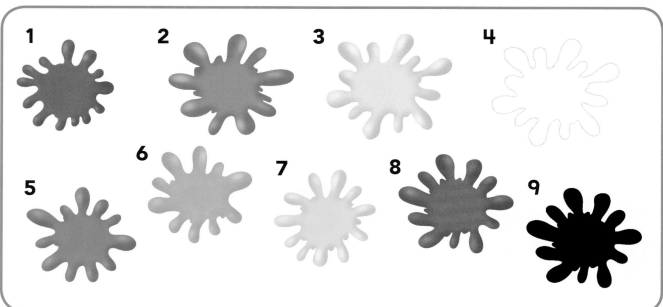

1   2   3   4

5   6   7   8   9

9 **Listen, look and say. Ask and answer.**

1   2   3

10 **Listen, look and say.**

1   2    3

4   5   6

11 **Listen and find. Play.**

12 🎧 1:14 **Listen, look and say. Do.**

1

2

3

4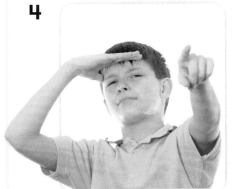

5

6

13 **Play.**

unit 1 My Family

1 Listen, look and say.

2 Listen and find.

3 Play a game.

4 Listen and find. Sing. 🎵

1:20

5 Listen and say yes or no.

1:21

1

2

3

4

THINK BIG Who's this? Say.

Story

6 1:23 **Listen and follow. Who's Liam?**

7 Look, listen and number.

Language in Action

Listen. Help Sam and Liam.

9 **Listen and ✓ or ✗.**

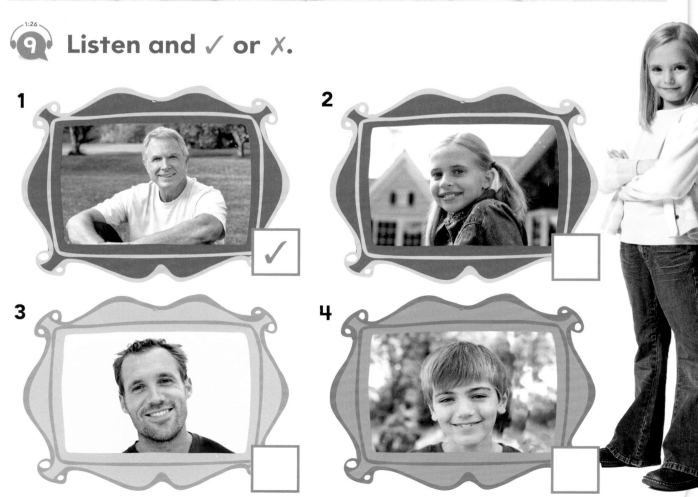

1:28

10 **Listen and number.**

11 **Draw and play.**

Listen and say.

1

2

3

4

THINK BIG Is my family big or small? Say.

1

2

1   **a**    **b**

2   **a**    **b**

3   **a**    **b**

Project

(14) **Make and say.**

15 Listen, look and say.

1

2

3

16 Look and ✓ or ✗.

1

2

3

17 Draw and say.

18 **Listen, find and say.** **19** **Listen and circle.**

 20 **Listen and number. Chant.**

a

b

21 Listen and follow.

22 Play.

1:38
23 Listen and ✓ or ✗.

1 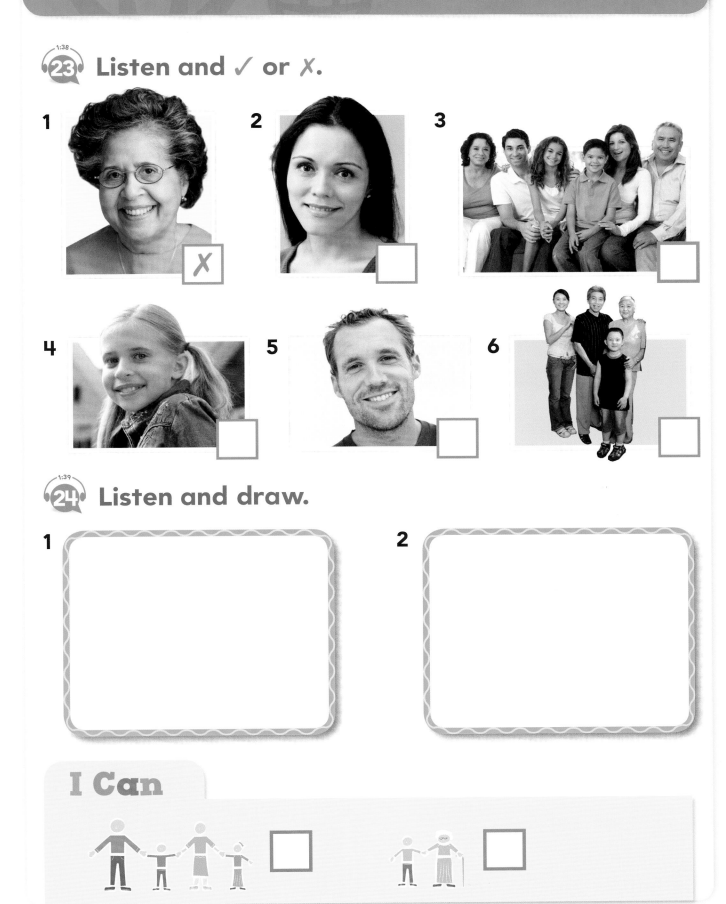 ✗

2

3

4

5

6

1:39
24 Listen and draw.

1

2

I Can

unit 2 Happy Birthday!

1 Listen, look and say.

2 Listen and find.

3 Play a game.

4 Listen and ✓. Sing. 🎵

1

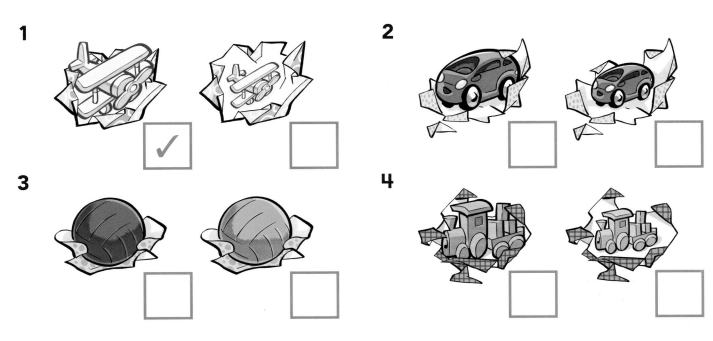

2

3

4

5 Find the differences.

1

2

THINK BIG Say the favourite toys.

1

2

Story

6 Listen and follow. What is each present?

7 Look and match. Say.

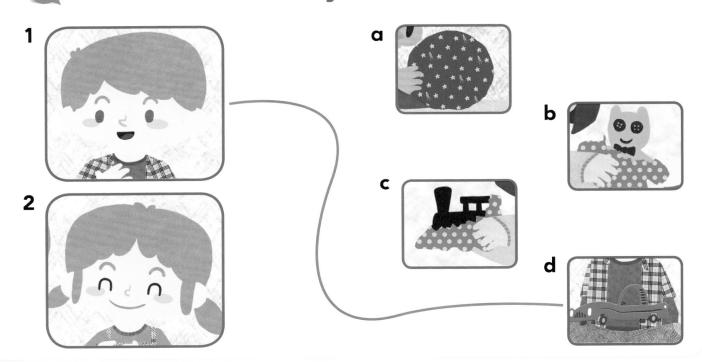

8 1:47 **Listen. Help Lidya and Liam.**

9 1:48 **Listen and circle.**

Listen and number. Ask and answer.

a  ☐

b  ☐

c  ☐

d  1

11 **Ask and draw.**

Me	1	2

Listen and say.

1

2

3

4

THINK BIG **Listen, number and say.**

a

b

c

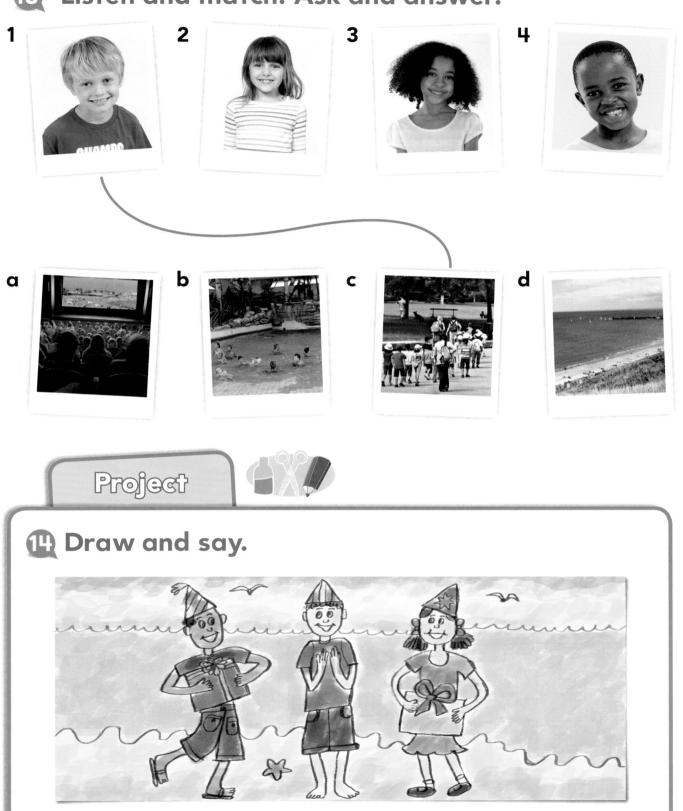

13 Listen and match. Ask and answer.

1:54

1   2   3   4

a   b   c   d

Project

14 Draw and say.

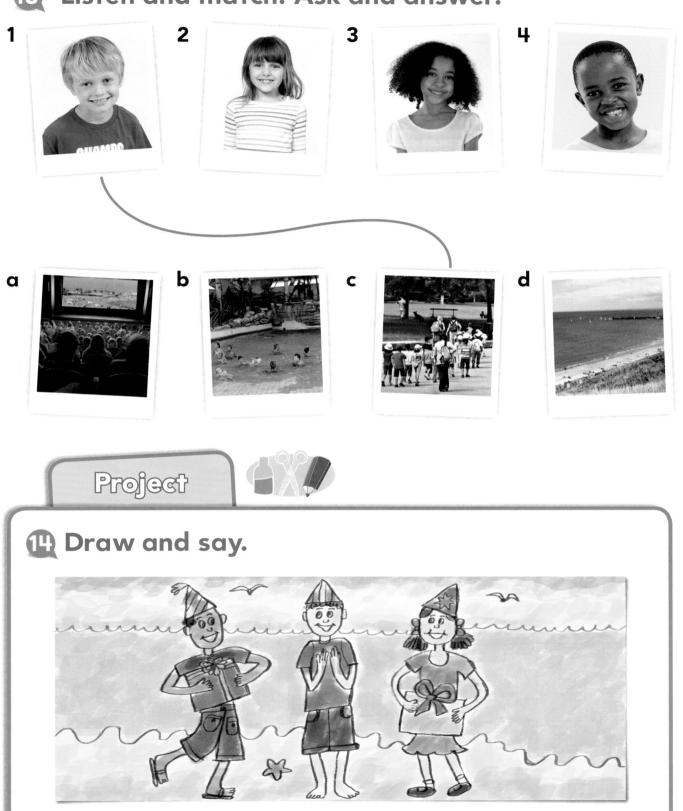

15 Listen and say.

1

2

16 Listen and find. Say.

17 Act and say.

18 Listen, find and say. **19** Listen and circle.

20 Listen and number. Chant.

a

b

c

Review

21 1:62 Listen and find.

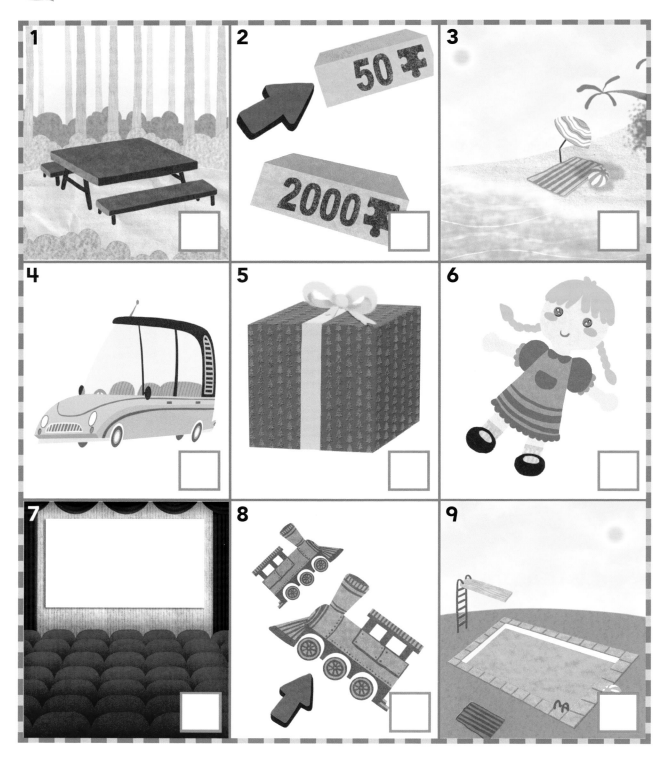

22 Play. Draw o or x.

23 **Listen and number.**

a

b

c  1

d

e

f

24 **Listen and draw.**

1

2

I Can

1 Listen, look and say.

4 Listen and ✓. Sing.

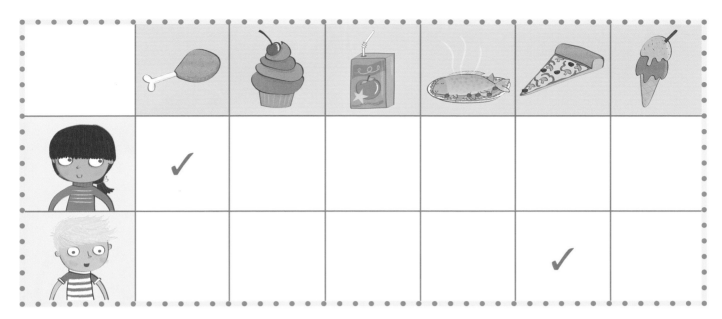

	(chicken)	(cupcake)	(juice)	(fish)	(pizza)	(ice cream)
(girl)	✓					
(boy)					✓	

5 Listen and draw.

THINK BIG Draw the food you like.

6 Listen and follow. What does each person like?

7 Look and listen again. Circle.

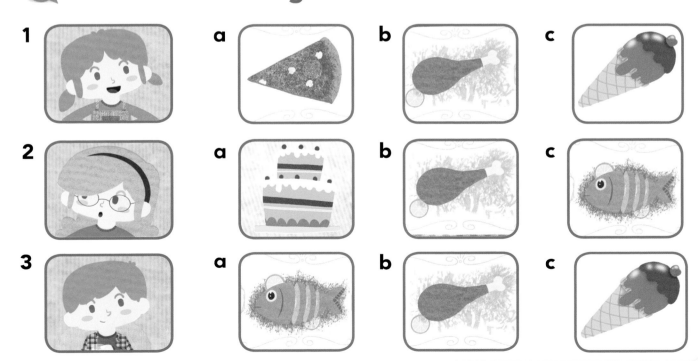

Listen. Help Lidya and Liam.

 Listen and circle.

1

2

3

4

10 Listen and ✓ or ✗. Say and guess.

1   2   3

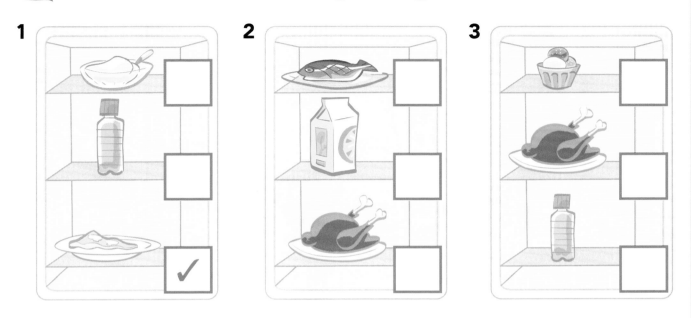

11 Play the game.

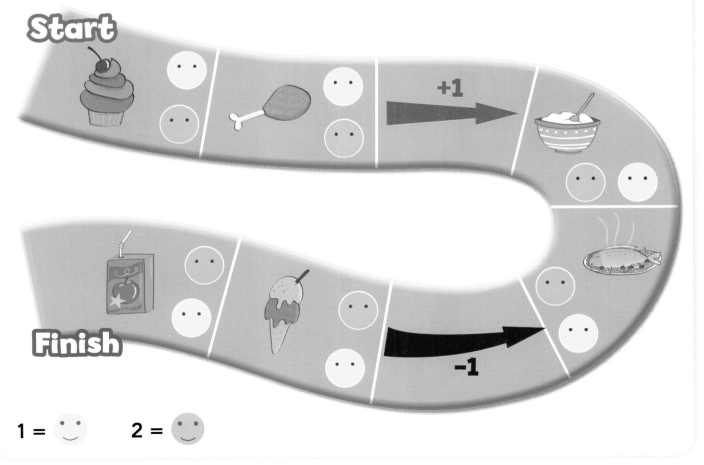

1 = 😊   2 = 🙂

Listen, look and say. Match.

1

2

3

4

THINK BIG Find the odd one out.

1

2

3

4

13 Draw and say.

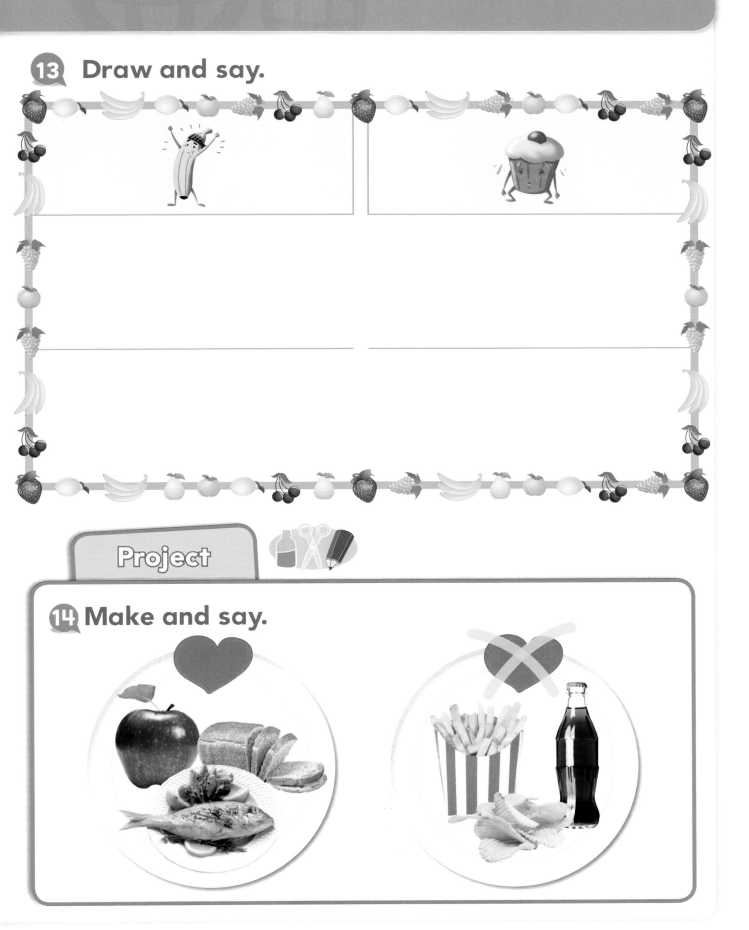

15 Listen, look and say. Draw.

1:80

1

2

3

4

16 Play Simon Says.   **17 Act and say.**

18 Listen, find and say. **19** Listen and circle.

20 Listen and number. Chant.

a

b

c

21 Listen and number.

a

b

c

d

e

1

f

22 Play.

1:86
23 **Listen and circle.**

1  ☺ ☹

2  ☺ ☹

3  ☺ ☹

4  ☺ ☹

5  ☺ ☹

6  ☺ ☹

24 **Draw and say.**

1 ☺

2 ☹

3 ♥

4 ✗

I Can

Do I Know It?

1 Look and circle. Practise.

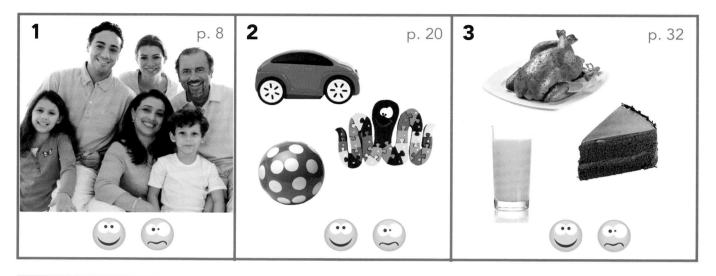

I Can Do It!

2 Listen and number.

3 Go to page 123. Cut.

 4 Listen and place. Play.

1	**2**	**3**
4	**5**	**6**

Do I Know It Now?

5 Draw and say.

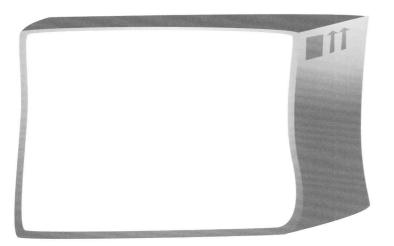

6 Think and draw.

1
2
3
4
5
6
7
8
9

My Body

1 Listen, look and say.

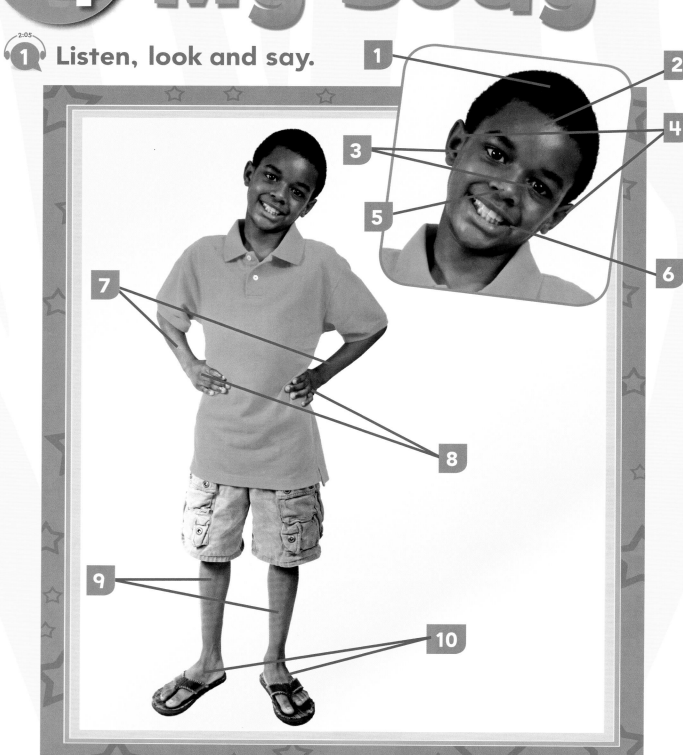

2 Listen and find.

3 Play a game.

4 Listen and find. Sing. 🎵

1 **2** **3**

5 Listen and number. Say and guess.

a **b** **c** **d**

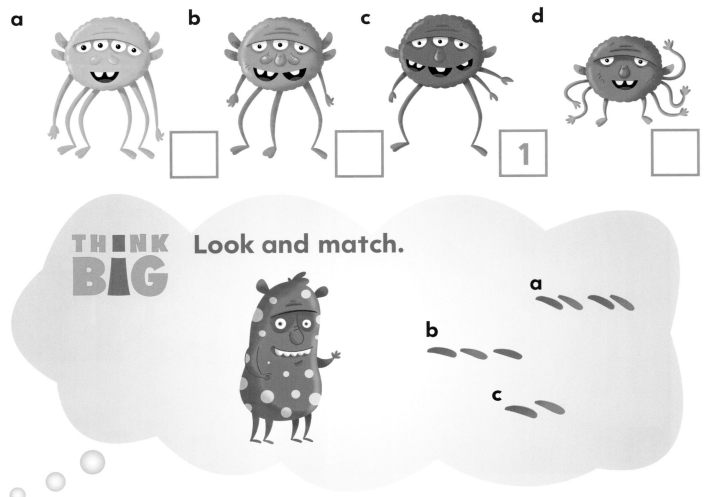

THINK BIG Look and match.

a

b

c

Story

6 Listen and follow. What colour is Lidya's nose?

🎧 **2:12**
7 Listen and colour. Look and circle.

1

2

8 Listen. Help Sally and Lidya.

9 Listen and number.

a

b

c

d

1

10 Listen, circle and ✓.

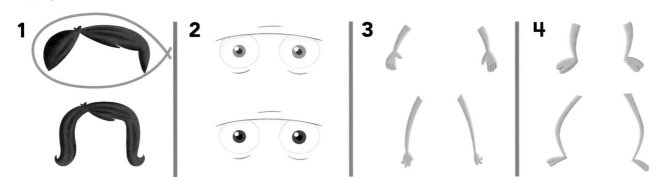

1   **2**   **3**   **4**

 **a**

 **b**

11 Draw. Ask and answer.

Number in order. Listen and say.

a

b

1

c

d

THINK BIG Look and draw.

1

2

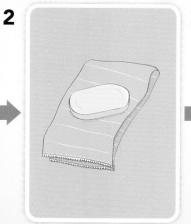

3

13 Choose and say.

Project

14 Make and say.

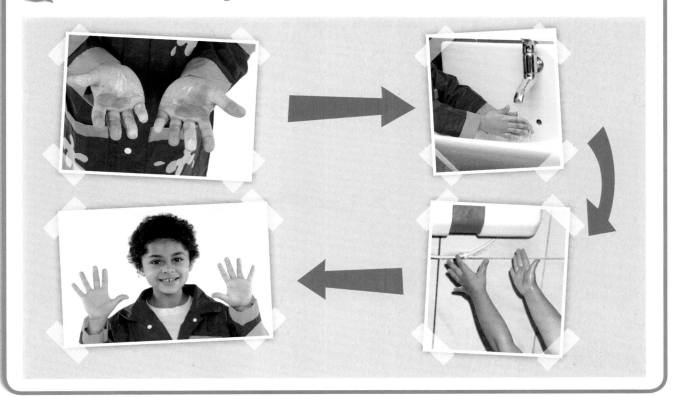

Values | Keep clean.

15 Listen, look and say.

1 　**2** 　**3**

16 Look and match. Say.

1 　**2** 　**3**

a 　**b** 　**c**

17 Act and say.

Listen, find and say. **Listen and circle.**

 **Listen and number. Chant.**

a

b

c

Listen and follow. Say the colour.

 **Play.**

23 Listen and ✓ or ✗.

1
 ✗

2

3

4

 24 Listen and number.

a

b

c

I Can

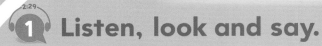

unit 5 Around Town

2:29

1 Listen, look and say.

2:30

2 Listen and find.

3 Play a game.

Listen and say the colour. Sing and do.

5 **Listen and match. Say and guess.**

1

2

3

4

a

b

c

d

THINK BIG **Say the places.**

1

2

6 Listen and follow. What's Lidya doing?

7 Listen and circle.

1 a    b

2 a    b

3 a    b

Language in Action

 2:37

8 Listen. Help Sam and Liam.

 2:38

9 Listen and match. Draw and say.

2:40

10 Listen and draw. Play.

1 2 3 4

5 6

x2

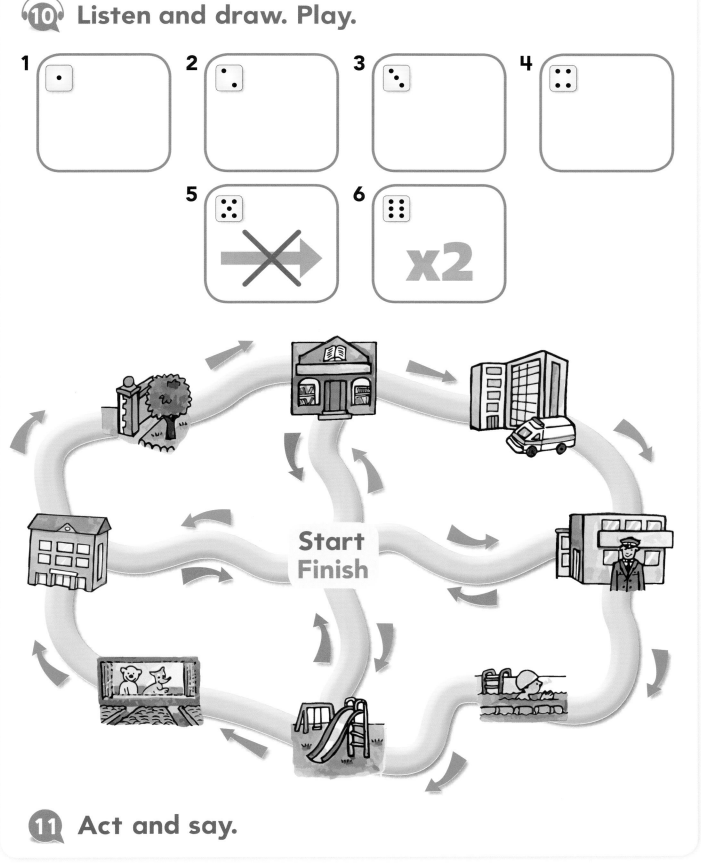

Start
Finish

11 Act and say.

language practice (*What's she doing? She's jumping to the park.*)   Unit 5   **63**

Listen, look and say.

1

2

3

4

5

THINK BIG Look and choose.

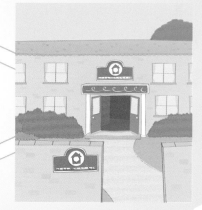

13 Match. Ask and answer.

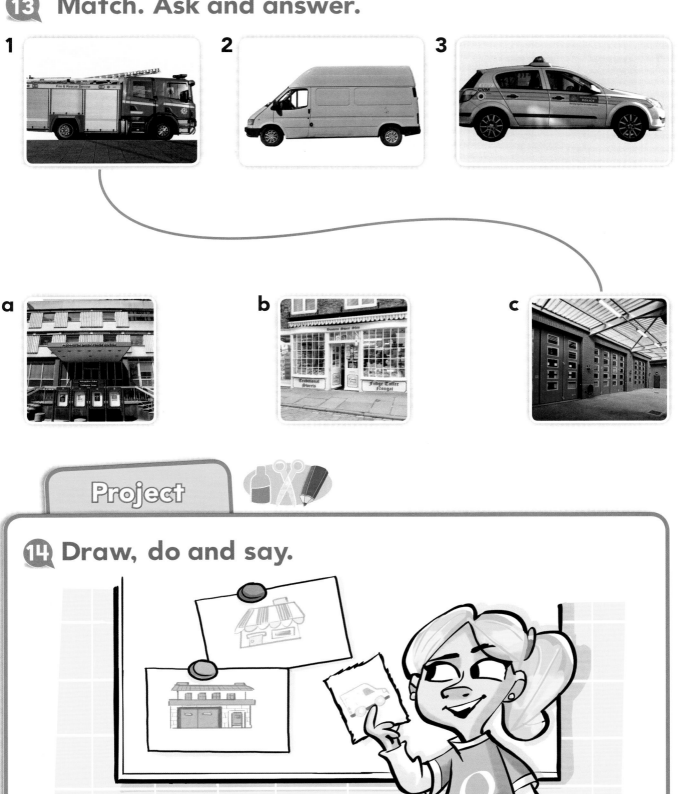

Project

14 Draw, do and say.

2:43
15 Look, listen and say.

1  **2**  **3**

16 Look and draw.

1

2

3

4

17 Show and say.

18 **Listen, find and say.** **19** **Listen and circle.**

20 **Listen and number. Chant.**

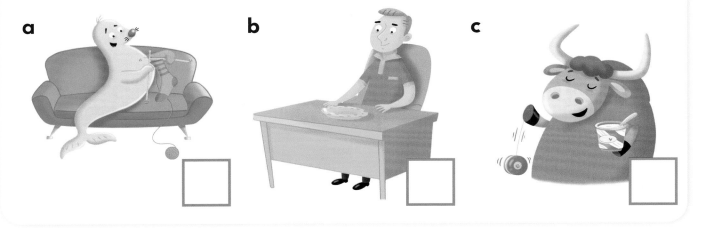

a

b

c

21 Listen and find.

22 Play. Draw o or x.

Listen and ✓ or ✗.

1  ✓

2

3

4

5

6

24 Draw and say.

1

2

I Can

  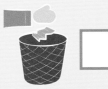

She's swinging on the swings!

2:50

1 Listen, look and say.

2:51

2 Listen and find.

3 Play a game.

Listen and number in order. Sing.

5 **Look at 4 and say.**

THINK BIG **Draw and say.**

1

2

3

4

Story

6 Listen and follow. What's Lidya doing wrong?

7 Look and ✓ or ✗.

1 a

b

2 a

b

Language in Action

2:56

8 Listen. Help Joy and Lidya.

2:57

9 Listen and circle.

1 a  b

2 a  b

3 a  b

4 a b

🎧 2:59 10 Listen and number. Say.

a

b

1

c

d

11 Mime and guess.

12 Listen, find and say.

1

2

3

4

THINK BIG What season is it? Say.

13 **Draw and say.**

 Project

14 **Make and say.**

15 Listen, look and say.

1  **2**  **3**  **4**

16 Look and ✓ or ✗. Say.

1  **2**  **3**  **4**

17 Draw.

18 Listen, find and say.   **19** Listen and circle.

20 Listen and number. Chant.

a

b

c

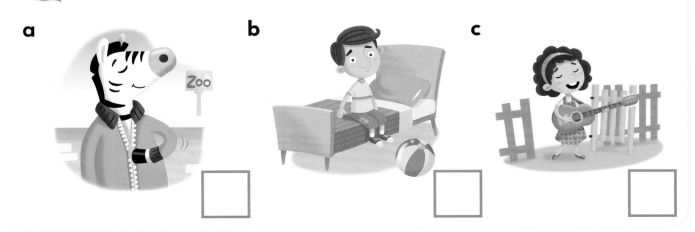

21 Look and number.

22 Play. Ask and answer. Then number.

23 Listen and number.

1

2

3

1

4

 **24 Listen and ✓ or ✗.**

1
 ✓

2

3

4

I Can

Checkpoint | Units 4–6

Do I Know It?

1 Look and circle. Practise.

| 1 | p. 46 | 2 | pp. 58–59 | 3 | p. 70 |

I Can Do It!

2 Listen and number.

2:69

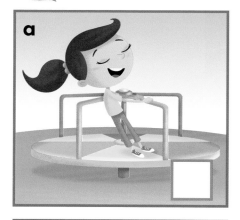

a

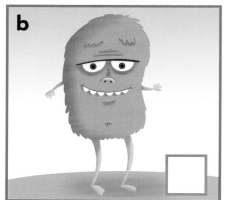

b

c

d

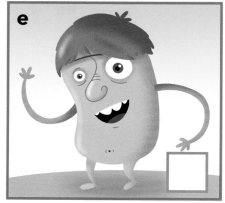

e

f   1

3 Go to page 125. Cut.

4 Listen and place. Play.

1	**2**	**3**
4	**5**	**6**

 **Do I Know It Now?**

5 Draw and say.

6 Think and draw.

It's sunny!

3:01

1 Listen, look and say.

3:02

2 Listen and find.

3 Play a game.

Listen and find. Sing. ♪

 Listen and number. Say.

a

b

c  `1`

d

THINK BIG   **Find the odd one out.**

6 Listen and follow. What's the weather like?

1

2

3

4

5

6

Listen and number.

a

b

c

8 Listen. Help Liam and Lidya.

9 Listen and circle.

1 a  **b**  **2 a**  **b**

3 a  **b**  **4 a**  **b**

3:12

10 Listen and ✓. Play.

1

2

3

4

11 Draw and say.

Listen, find and say.

1

2

3

4

THINK BIG **Listen and look. Draw and say.**

1

2

13 Look and match. Say.

1  **2** **3** **4**

a **b** **c** **d**

Project

14 Make and say.

15 Look and match. Listen and say.

1

a

2

b

3

c

16 Look at 15. Draw.

17 Show and say.

18 Listen, find and say.   19 Listen and circle. ✏️

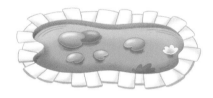

20 Listen and number. Chant.

a

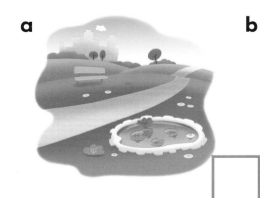

b

c

phonics (*c*, *p*, *h*) Unit 7   **93**

Review

3:21

21 Listen and follow. Say the colour.

22 Play.

23 Listen and ✓ or ✗.

1

✗

2

3

4

24 Listen and draw.

1

2

I Can

 □    □    □

My House

1 Listen, look and say.

2 Listen and find.

3 Play a game.

Listen and sing. Number in order. ♪

 Listen and circle. Say the room.

1 a   b   2 a   b

3 a   b   4 a   b

THINK BIG   **Find the odd one out.**

6 Listen and follow. Where's Lidya?

7 Listen and ✓ or ✗.

1

✓

2

3

4

Listen. Help Lidya and Liam.

 Listen and match.

1

2

3

4

a

b

c

d

10 **Draw Liam, Joy and you. Ask and answer.**

11 **Ask and answer. Where are you?**

Me			
1			
2			
3			

Listen, find and say.

1

2

3

4

THINK BIG What lives here?

13 Match and draw. Say.

1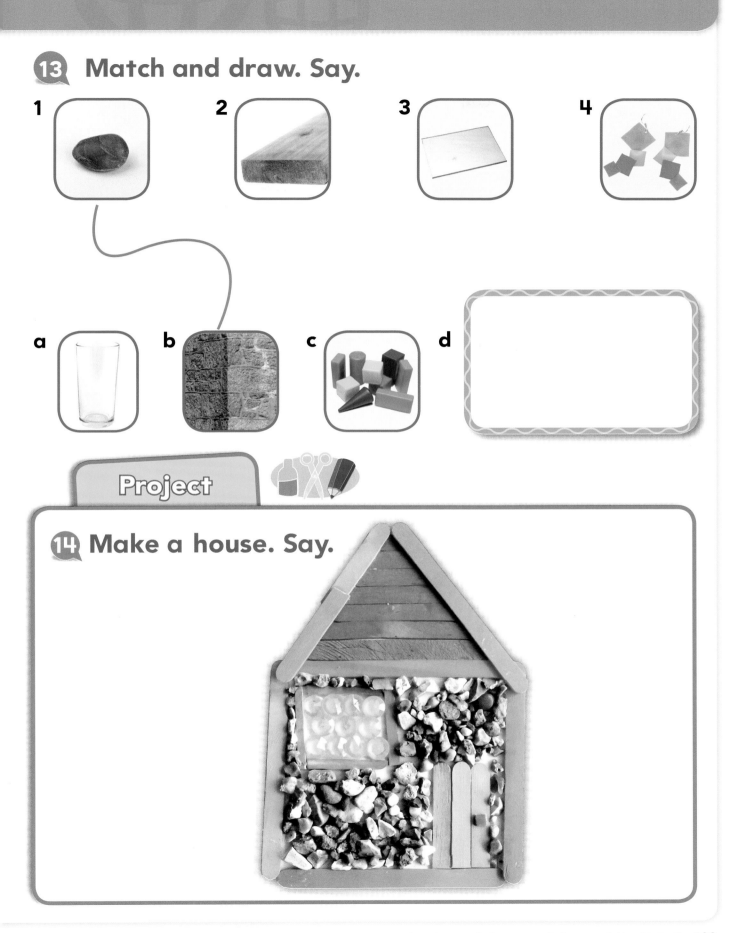
2
3
4

a
b
c
d

Project

14 Make a house. Say.

15 Listen, look and say.

1

2

3

4

16 Look and ✓ or ✗. Say.

1

2

3

17 Draw and act.

Listen, find and say. **Listen and circle.**

 Listen and number. Chant.

a

b

c

21 Listen and find.

1

2

3

4

5

6

7

8

9

22 Play. Draw x or o.

Listen and number.

a

b

c  **1**

d

 Listen and draw.

I Can

unit 9 A fish can swim!

🎧 **1** Listen, look and say.

🎧 **2** Listen and find.

💬 **3** Play a game.

4 **Listen and sing. What's missing?** 🎵

5 **Listen and number. Say.**

1

TH NK BIG **What can it do?**

1

2

3

6 Listen and follow. Where's Lidya?

7 Look and ✓ or ✗. Say.

1  ✓

2

3

4

Listen. Help Lidya and Liam.

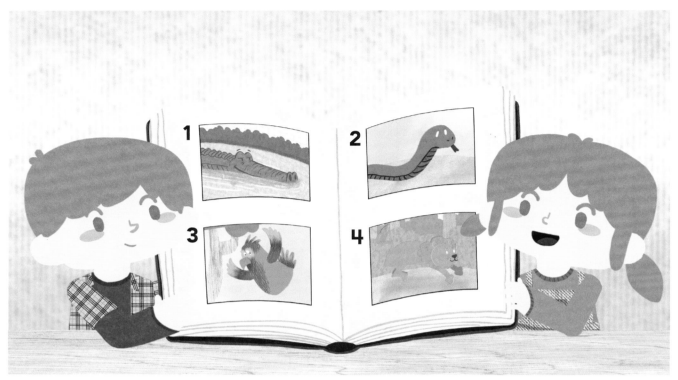

 Circle ✓ or ✗. Listen and check.

10 Listen and play.

11 Draw and say.

Listen, look and say.

1

2

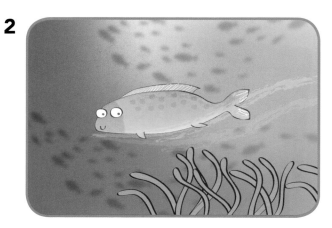

3

4

THINK BIG What's wrong?

1

2

13 **Look and match. Say.**

1

2

3

4

a

b

c

d

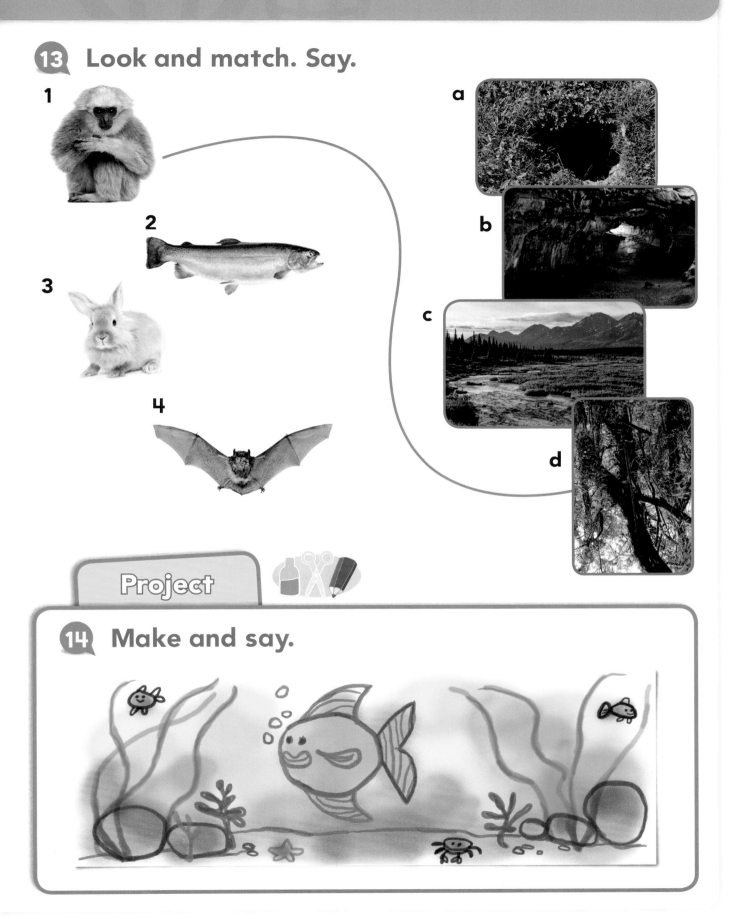

Project

14 **Make and say.**

15 Listen, look and say.

1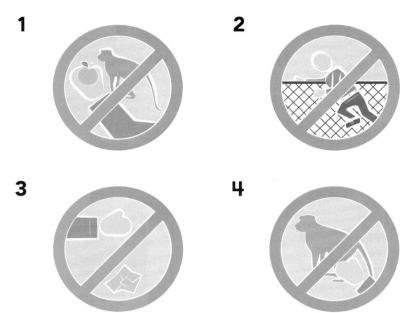

2

3

4

16 Look and circle. Say the rule.

17 Act and say.

18 Listen, find and say.　**19** Listen and circle.

20 Listen and number. Chant.

a

b

c

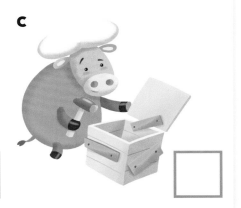

21 Listen and ✓ or ✗. Play.

	(climbing)	(hang gliding)	(swimming)	(running)
1	✓	✗		
2	✓	✗		
3	✗		✓	
4			✓	✗

Listen and match.

1

2

3

4

a

b

c

d

 Listen and number.

a

b

c **1**

d

I Can

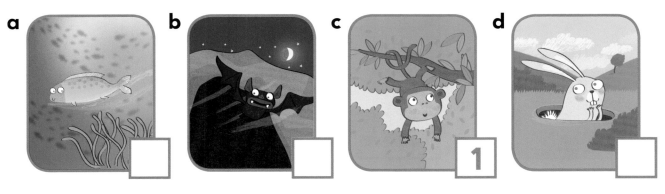

Checkpoint | Units 7–9

Do I Know It?

1 Look and circle. Practise.

| 1 | p. 84 | 2 | p. 96 | 3 | p. 108 |

I Can Do It!

2 Listen and number.

3 Go to page 127. Cut.

4 Listen and place. Play.

3:69

1

1	2	3
4	5	6

Do I Know It Now?

5 Draw and say.

6 Think and draw.

1

2

3

4

5

6

7

8

9